Tallow chandler. From the 'Book of English Trades and Library of the Useful Arts', London 1806.

CANDLE LIGHTING

David J. Eveleigh

Shire Publications Ltd

CONTENTS

Published in 2003 by Shire Publications Ltd, Cromwell House, Church Street, Princes Risborough, Buckinghamshire HP27 9AA, UK. Website: www.shirebooks.co.uk Copyright © 1985 and 2003 by David J. Eveleigh. First published 1985; reprinted 1991 and 1995. Second edition 2003. Shire Album 132. ISBN 0 7478 0574 1

Printed in Great Britain by CIT Printing Services Ltd, Press Buildings, Merlins Bridge, Haverfordwest, Pembrokeshire SA61 1XF.

British Library Cataloguing in Publication Data: Eveleigh, David J. Candle Lighting. – (Shire albums; 132). 1. Candles – History. I. Title. 621.3'23 ISBN 0 7478 0574 1.

ACKNOWLEDGEMENTS
Illustrations are acknowledged as follows: the Museum of English Rural Life, University of Reading, pages 1, 6 (left and right), 9, 11 (lower right), 12 (upper right), 14, 15 (upper and centre), 18 (upper), 19, 20 (right), 21, 23 (upper left and right and lower), 24 (upper and centre), 25 (lower), 27, 28, 29 (upper left and right), 30, 31 (left); Blaise Castle House Museum, City of Bristol Museum and Art Gallery, pages 3, 6 (centre), 8, 11 (lower left), 12 (all except upper right), 13, 15 (lower), 17, 18 (lower), 20 (left), 23 (upper centre), 24 (lower), 25 (upper right), 29 (lower), 31 (right); Country Quest, page 4 (lower right); the Welsh Folk Museum, pages 4 (upper and lower left), 5, 7; the Ironbridge Gorge Museum Trust, page 9. Special thanks are due to Ron Mason for the cover illustration and to Jane Jefferies for typing the manuscript. For the second edition, thanks are due to Robert A. C. Duff for his comments on some of the captions.

COVER: *Candlelighting appliances from Blaise Castle House Museum, City of Bristol Museum and Art Gallery. From left, brass candlestick (c.1750), tinplate lantern, brass snuffers, tinplate candlestick, brass chamberstick and wrought iron combined rush and candle holder.*

Twelve modern paraffin wax candles on a Flemish-style brass chandelier of the early eighteenth century illuminate the study of the Georgian House Museum, Bristol.

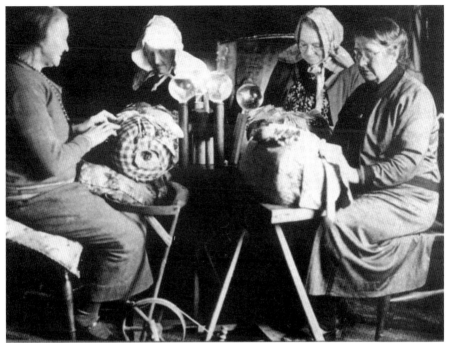

Some domestic handcrafts, knitting and straw plaiting for example, were simple and repetitive enough to be done by the light of the fire. Lacemaking, though, demanded good light. Here, lacemakers are working by the light of a single candle, magnified and multiplied by clear glass globes, filled with water. Variously known as a lacemaker's 'condenser', a 'candle-block' and a 'flash', this device is recorded as early as the late sixteenth century.

INTRODUCTION

A typical dictionary definition of a candle – that is, a light made of a solid fuel surrounding a wick of flax or cotton – gives no indication of the fascinating story that lies behind this simple form of lighting. For over two thousand years, the candle has proved one of the most successful and reliable forms of artificial light. Candles appear to have been used in ancient Egypt as early as 300 BC while the Roman historian Pliny described how rushes could be used to make the wicks of lights.

Candles have been used in every possible situation. In Saxon England, King Alfred gave instructions for making candles that could be used to mark the hours of the day. Candles also have a strong association with churches and religious services. Other important ceremonies were lit by candles: the coronation celebrations for George III, for example, at Westminster Hall in 1761 were

illuminated by three thousand wax candles. People on the move used candle lamps or lanterns but the greatest use of candles was in the home, where candles were burned in many different types of candlesticks and other holders.

Candle lighting reached its peak of development in the mid nineteenth century: there were sixty-four exhibitors of candles from across the world at the Great Exhibition in 1851. The range was vast, with candles made of several different materials. There were candles with self-fitting ends, candles for carriage and reading lamps that burned in special sprung tubes, night lights and candles for pianos. They were made coloured, fluted, twisted – and then there the tiny candles for birthday cakes and Christmas trees. But the manufacturers' greatest achievement was to develop bright and efficient candles that everyone could afford.

3

ABOVE: *Gathering rushes, Meirionydd, Gwynedd, North Wales, 1977.*
BELOW, LEFT: *Peeling a rush.*
BELOW, RIGHT: *Drawing the rushes through molten fat, using a hanging frying pan, at Abergeirw, Meirionydd, Gwynedd, in 1953.*

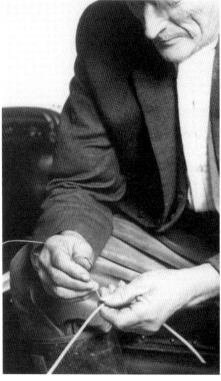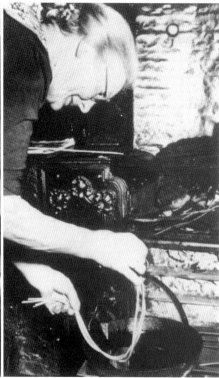

Melting the fat over the fire in a grisset for rushlight making at Cwm Cywarch, near Dinas Mawddwy, Meirionydd, Gwynedd, in 1977.

RUSHLIGHTS

The simplest form of candle was the *rushlight*, made by drawing a rush through waste kitchen fat. In 1673 John Aubrey, the antiquarian, reported that the inhabitants of Ockley in Surrey made their own rushlights, and Gilbert White described the preparation in detail in his *Natural History of Selborne* (1775). Scattered evidence for their use in other parts of Britain suggests that rushlights were used locally wherever the common soft rush, *Juncus effusus*, was to be found. They continued to be used in some rural areas of England until late in the nineteenth century, but in Wales the tradition still lingered in the mid twentieth century.

Late summer was the best time to collect the rushes. By then they had attained their full height but were still green. The ends were cut off leaving a rush about 18 inches (460 mm) long. The skin was peeled off — an operation which called for some manual dexterity, leaving a single strip of skin to support the soft pith. When the rushes had dried, kitchen fat was melted in a wide boat-shaped pan called a *grisset*. These were made of either wrought or cast iron and supplied with legs so they could stand in the fire. Several rushes were then carefully drawn through the liquid fat until the pith was completely soaked. Finally the rushes were put out to dry on pieces of bark, which, according to William Cobbett's *Cottage Economy* of 1821, were sometimes strapped to the wall so that the rushlights could be stored.

Rushlights were burned in specially made holders with jaws which held the rush at roughly 45 degrees. About 1½ inches (38 mm) was drawn through at a time; on average a rushlight would burn for between fifteen and twenty minutes. Rushlight holders were never mass-produced but were individually made in wrought iron by local blacksmiths. Surviving examples often exhibit considerable grace and variety of form.

In 1709 an Act of Parliament banned the making of candles at home unless a licence was purchased and a tax was

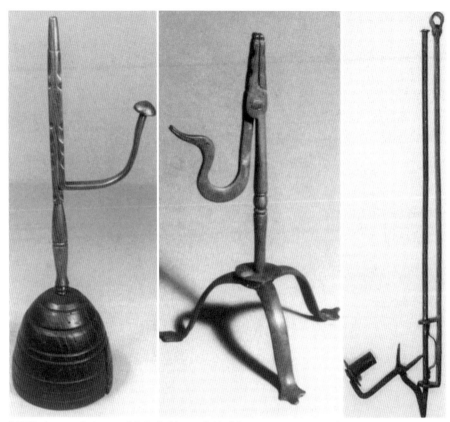

LEFT: *A wrought iron rushlight holder with filed decoration on a turned wooden base, probably from central Wales.*
RIGHT: *A rushlight holder on a tripod base with decoration characteristic of holders from mid or north-west Wales.*
RIGHT: *An adjustable hanging rush and candle holder of wrought iron.*

imposed on candles. Rushlights, however, were excluded from the terms of the Act and so became by far the cheapest form of candle lighting. Gilbert White examined the economics of candle lighting and calculated that, whereas a half-penny candle gave little more than two hours light, for a farthing rushlights sufficient to produce five and a half hours light could be had. Yet White lamented the fact that in spite of this considerable saving the poor continued to buy expensive candles. This he attributed to their poor sense of economics, but William Cobbett appreciated that the diet of the poor had some bearing on this problem. In 1821 he wrote: 'Candles certainly were not much used in English Labourers' dwellings in the days when they had meat dinners and Sunday coats.' To Cobbett the increasing impoverishment of the agricultural labourer meant less meat (and no best clothes), and in turn less surplus fat with which to make rushlights. Later in the nineteenth century, investigations into the living conditions of farm labourers revealed that their diet was often lacking in meat. For a family which perhaps ate only a little bacon once a week there was no such notion as waste fat; instead it was called dripping and eaten with bread. If a labourer wanted light he had to buy a candle. The same investigations into living standards showed that candles often formed a significant item in the weekly budget of labourers' families for about half the year.

6

Making tallow dips on Bank Farm, Abergorlech, Carmarthenshire, 1901.

TALLOW CANDLES

Ordinary candles for everyday use were made of tallow, which is simply animal fat separated from the membranous matter which might putrefy. Most animals yield tallow, but candlemakers usually took the fat from bullocks and sheep. Bullock or *beef tallow* comprised the fat of oxen, cows and bulls. Sheep or *mutton tallow* was obtained from rams, ewes, bucks and she-goats and was valued by chandlers for its gloss and hardness. Generally the cheaper candles were made solely of beef tallow while the better quality kinds contained roughly equal portions of beef and mutton tallow. It was not unknown for the very cheapest to include pig's fat, which produced a foul-smelling, thick black smoke.

In areas of mixed or pastoral farming, tallow was a readily available commodity and traditionally it was the duty of the farmer's wife to make candles for the home. After 1709 this was forbidden by Act of Parliament, but evidence for the domestic production of candles during the sixteenth and seventeenth centuries is relatively sparse. Farmhouse inventories for this period provide ample evidence for the domestic production of butter, cheese, beer and many other commodities but rarely list the materials and equipment necessary for candle-making. Contrary to popular tradition, most farmers, it would seem, were content to buy their candles. Cottagers, the very poor and town dwellers had no choice for they were usually without sufficient fat to make candles.

There are instances, however, of men who combined farming with candle-making. John Elford, for example, a farmer of Chetnole in north Dorset, died in 1637 leaving not only dairy cattle but a workshop containing tallow, wicks and candle moulds. He probably supplied the neighbouring farms and cottages with all the candles they required. There were others like John Elford, and candlemakers or *chandlers* were to be found in virtually every market town, and many villages besides. Nevertheless, in remote areas where communities had to be more self-sufficient, candles were made at home. Samuel Johnson, for instance, saw candles made in every house on the Isle of Coll whilst on his tour of the Hebrides in 1773. As late as 1930 candles continued to be made domestically on some isolated farms in Powys, Wales; tallow sufficient for three years was obtained by the slaughter of one bullock although other farms relied on mutton tallow.

Remote areas apart, candlemaking was an old and long established industry. In London, both the wax chandlers and the tallow chandlers had formed their own guilds before the end of the fifteenth century. The industry was often highly localised. Nearby farms and slaughter-houses provided the raw material and there was always an assured local market. By the eighteenth century local supplies were being supplemented by Russian tallow, which was imported in large quantities. Nevertheless, the majority of chandlers still undertook the noisome and laborious task of rendering tallow.

A tallow chandler dipping wicks on a broach into a trough of liquid fat. From the 'Universal Magazine of Knowledge and Pleasure', 1749.

For this operation the essential piece of equipment was a large cauldron, or boiler, made of iron or copper, in which the tallow was melted. Not only was this a smelly process, but there was also a risk of fire should the tallow boil over. To avert this danger the boilers were often fitted with a cavity around the top rim to catch any escaping tallow. Once the fat had melted, the cellular membrane, skin and other waste material rose to the surface and were skimmed off. Remaining impurities were separated by the addition of water, which caused them to settle in a layer between the water and the fat. The tallow was then ready to be strained into storage tubs. Finally, the residue was placed in a press to extract any final tallow. The cake produced by this operation, *greave*, was fed to dogs, pigs and, in the Vale of Aylesbury, ducks.

The first stage of candlemaking was the preparation of the wick. Tallow candles had wicks made of several strands of spun cotton, which was bought in large balls or skeins. Three or four or more threads, depending on the thickness of the intended candle, were wound together and cut to the length required on a cutting board. This simple device had an adjustable peg at one end around which the cotton was doubled, and cutting blade at the other. As the blade cut the wick it added a slight twist. So that the candle would burn without undue spluttering, the wicks were straightened and pulled free of knots; this operation was called *pulling the cotton.*

The cheapest tallow candles were known as *dips* after the method of making. The chandler prepared dipped candles by arranging a number of wicks on rods termed *broaches,* which were about 3 feet (1 m) long. Holding the broach at each end, the chandler then lowered the wicks into a rectangular vessel filled with molten tallow. The wicks were raised, coated with a thin layer of tallow. They were then hung on a rack until the tallow had sufficiently hardened to retain a new coat on fresh immersion. This operation was repeated until the candles had reached the required thickness. Finally, the peaked ends were removed by passing them over a heated brass plate.

A nineteenth-century dipping frame. Note the weights balancing the candles at the other end. From George Virtue's 'Cyclopedia of the Useful Arts', 1851.

According to a description of 1749, the chandler would dip up to three broaches simultaneously, but it was nonetheless a slow and laborious business. However, the invention of the *dipping frame* in the late eighteenth century greatly increased the number of candles which could be dipped at a time. This device consisted of a suspended wooden frame with an arched head at each end to give a vertical motion to the dipping. At one end approximately five broaches were held by two lengths of wood and they were balanced at the other end by weights equal to the finished candles. By means of this simple aid the operator had only to guide the broaches, and not to support their weight as in the earlier method. Nevertheless, skill was still required to keep the broaches horizontal so that the candles attained a uniform thickness. During the early nineteenth century several improved types of dipping machine were introduced. One of the most successful of these consisted of a revolving iron frame which maintained the broaches in a horizontal position regardless of undue pressure from the operator.

Superior to the humble dip were *mould candles*. These are generally thought to have originated in France during the fifteenth century. It is more certain that they were being made by English chandlers in the early seventeenth century, for by then candle moulds were recorded in inventories. The mould gave the candle a more finished and regular appearance than was possible by dipping. They were also made with better quality tallows as the cheaper types were too sticky to be used in the moulds. Candle moulds were often made by pewterers, although in the eighteenth century tinned iron ones became common. They took the form of a number of cylinders with conical ends set in a trough which was supported by a frame. Moulds varied in detail, but common to the successful operation of all was the necessity of ensuring that the wick remained tight and central whilst the hot tallow was added. The conical end of the mould had a hole through which the wick was inserted. At the other end the wick was usually doubled or looped so that a wire could hold it in place. Sometimes, when the mould was half filled, the chandler paused to ensure that the wick was still central before completely filling the mould. The candles were removed

Interior of a candle factory from Madeley, Shropshire, which has been reconstructed as a working exhibit at Blists Hill Museum, Ironbridge. This factory operated from about 1850 until 1930 and made tallow dips on a dipping frame known as the 'nodding donkey'. It took about twenty dips to make a candle on this machine and as many as thirty thousand candles were produced each week. Chandlers often hung candles from the ceiling so they were out of the reach of rats.

from the moulds once they had set and were then left to bleach so that they would more resemble their expensive wax counterparts. Some chandlers dipped the wicks of mould candles in beeswax as a further refinement.

Diaries and account books occasionally record payments for candles. A market book belonging to Francis Prior, a gentleman farmer of Ufton, Berkshire, includes a typical purchase from a Reading chandler in January 1788: 'Bot. and paid for a Doz. of candles 10 in the pound of Mr Lamb, High Street, 8s 6d.' As this record indicates, candles were usually sold by the pound (0.45 kg). There were three principal sizes, *eights,* of which eight made a pound, *tens,* the type bought by Prior on this occasion, and *twelves,* which were the least substantial, being twelve to a pound. Prior's candles cost him 8½d per pound and were subject to candle tax. This was repealed in 1831, and in the mid nineteenth century the cheapest dips sold for 6d a pound, while wax candles, always the most expensive, were over 2 shillings per pound.

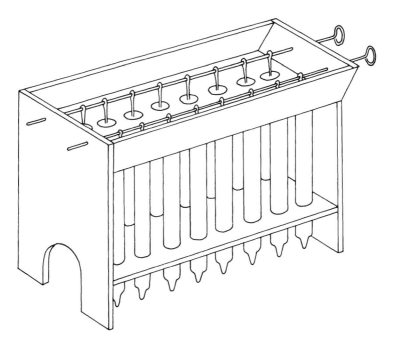

ABOVE: *A moulding frame showing the wires inserted through the loops of the wicks to keep them tight and central. Redrawn from an engraving in 'The Cyclopedia or Universal Dictionary of Arts, Sciences and Literature' by Abraham Rees, 1819.*

BELOW, LEFT: *Trade card of B. Vines, soap and candle maker of Bristol, c 1823-47, advertising 'fine mould candles'. It was common to find the trades of soap and candle making combined as both used tallow and vegetable oils.*

BELOW, RIGHT: *A tinplate candle mould to make twelve candles.*

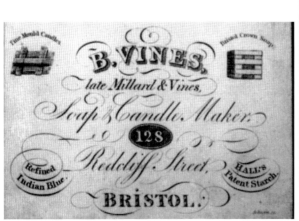

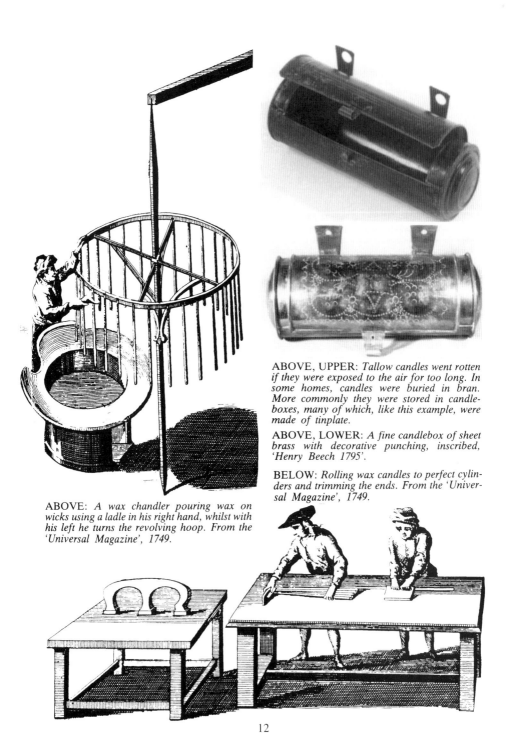

ABOVE, UPPER: *Tallow candles went rotten if they were exposed to the air for too long. In some homes, candles were buried in bran. More commonly they were stored in candle-boxes, many of which, like this example, were made of tinplate.*

ABOVE, LOWER: *A fine candlebox of sheet brass with decorative punching, inscribed, 'Henry Beech 1795'.*

BELOW: *Rolling wax candles to perfect cylinders and trimming the ends. From the 'Universal Magazine', 1749.*

ABOVE: *A wax chandler pouring wax on wicks using a ladle in his right hand, whilst with his left he turns the revolving hoop. From the 'Universal Magazine', 1749.*

Another view from the 'Universal Magazine', showing two men making wax tapers. The chafing dish of hot coals to keep the wax liquid can clearly be seen.

BEESWAX AND SPERMACETI CANDLES

Candles made from *beeswax* have a long history of use in churches, but they were also used in the home by those who could afford them, being far superior to tallow candles. In 1663 Samuel Pepys tried them, 'to see', he wrote, 'whether the smoke offends like that of tallow candles'. Beeswax candles were indeed a lot less smoky. They also burned with a brighter flame and without the unpleasant smell which accompanied tallow candles.

Beeswax was obtained from honeycomb by a simple process of melting and straining to remove impurities; this yielded a yellow wax with an unmistakable smell of honey. For candlemaking the wax was usually bleached. This was done by remelting the wax and passing it through a tub with a perforated bottom, which separated the wax into thin strips. These were then laid out in the open on linen cloths and exposed to the action of the sun for several weeks. Much of the beeswax used by British wax chandlers was imported from abroad, although they often carried out the final refining themselves. In Britain the bleaching was subject to the vagaries of the weather. Attempts to quicken the process in the early nineteenth century by using chlorine proved unsuccessful as the wax was rendered too brittle.

According to R. Campbell, author of *The London Tradesman* (1747), the business of the wax chandler was 'more profitable than that of the tallow chandler, and reckoned a more genteel trade'. Wax chandlers were further distinguished by their own specialist techniques. Beeswax could not be used in moulds because it contracted on cooling and also because it stuck tenaciously to the sides of the mould. Some wax candles were made by wrapping pieces of wax around a wick by hand, but generally the wax was applied with a ladle. As many as thirty or forty wicks were tied to a revolving iron hoop suspended over a large cauldron of melted wax and heated by a small fire underneath. Using a ladle, the workman poured hot wax down the sides of the wick, one by one, until the required thickness was obtained. Whilst they were still warm and soft, the candles were rolled to perfect cylinders on an even surface using rollers of a hard wood, such as box or lignum vitae. So that the wax would not stick to the roller, it was necessary to keep it moist with hot water.

Thin wax tapers, sometimes referred to as *bougies,* were made by a process called *drawing* from its similarity to wire drawing. A considerable length of wick was wound around two large wooden rollers, which were placed either side of a basin of melted wax. By turning the rollers the wick was drawn through the melted wax and at the same time through two perforated iron plates with cylindrical holes, which determined the final thickness. This device is reputed to have originated in Venice and spread to Paris and London in the mid seventeenth century. The same process was still in use at the Lambeth Marsh works of J. C. and J. Field in 1862, when 'The Iron-monger' reported that between 10 and 12 miles (16-19 km) of bougies were manufactured each week.

During the first half of the eighteenth century it was discovered that candles could be made from an oil present in the head cavities of sperm whales. One ordinary sized whale would yield nearly one ton of this substance, called *sper-maceti*, in a crude state. The crude sper-maceti was put into cloth bags and pressed to remove all the oil. It was then broken into pieces and boiled in water, which separated the impurities. Upon cooling, the spermaceti was again boiled in water, but this time with the addition of a weak solution of potash to remove the remaining oil. The resulting pure spermaceti was a hard white mass with a beautiful, flaky crystalline appearance, which characterised candles made of this substance. Spermaceti candles burned with a bright white flame which was taken as the standard unit of light in photometry. They were made in moulds but were only a little cheaper than wax candles.

GUTTERING AND SNUFFING

It was important to match the wick to the size of the candle; basically, the larger the candle, the larger the wick. But wick size was also governed by the melting point of the material from which the candle was made, and both these factors in turn affected the way the finished product burned. Wax and spermaceti had relatively high melting points, 68 degrees Celsius (154 Fahrenheit) and 55 degrees Celsius (131 Fahrenheit) respectively. Therefore the candle material melted slowly and so a small wick sufficed to draw this up to the flame. Tallow, with the much lower melting point of 33 degrees

A wax taper box of japanned iron. Tapers were largely used to melt sealing wax used for envelopes.

14

A pair of plain wrought iron snuffers. Similar examples were made in brass.

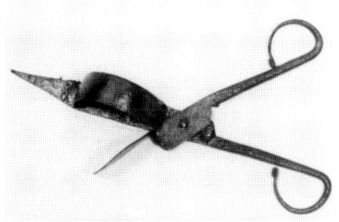

Hobday's snuffers, made without springs or levers, as specified in his second patent of 1818. These snuffers, like most mechanical types, were made of polished steel.

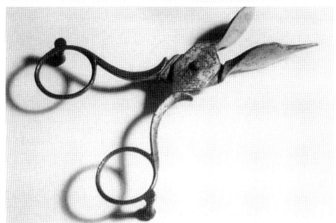

Douters, not to be confused with snuffers, used to extinguish the flame by nipping the wick. This pair is made of steel.

Celsius (91 Fahrenheit), was much more troublesome. Candles made of tallow quickly produced a large amount of hot fat and, unless they were supplied with a sufficiently large wick, excess fat ran down the sides of the candle, a fault known as *guttering*.

So tallow candles were always made with bulky wicks consisting of several strands of loosely twisted cotton. Unfortunately, these were the cause of further problems. The large wick produced a correspondingly large flame, which, starved of oxygen in the middle, was inclined to smoke owing to the escape of unburnt carbon. The small wicks of wax and spermaceti candles were usually given a tighter twist, by which means they tended to bend over towards the outside of the flame, where they burned away. But the wicks of tallow candles were too large to be consumed by the flame. As the candle gradually diminished, the wick in turn lengthened, gathering unburnt carbon, which considerably dimmed the brightness of the flame. At the very worst, the trailing wick dropped over the side of the candle causing more guttering.

Guttering was not only messy and unsightly but wasteful, for as much as half the candle could be lost this way. It was necessary, therefore, at intervals to trim the wicks of burning tallow candles. This operation was called *snuffing*. Specially adapted scissors known as *snuffers* were devised for this purpose. They are recorded in the privy purse expenses at the court of Henry VIII (reigned 1509-47), but they begin to appear in the inventories of ordinary homes only towards the close of the seventeenth century. Expensive snuffers with matching stands were made in silver, but most were made of either brass or iron. The earlier types were fitted with a box on each blade to take the charred wick or *snuff*. Snuffers of the eighteenth and nineteenth centuries had a single box with a flat press on the other blade which carried the snuff into the box and extinguished it. Unfortunately, when the snuffers were next used the old wick ends invariably fell out of the box. Benjamin Cartwright, a steel toy maker of the Strand, was the first to tackle this problem. In 1749 he took out a patent for a pair of mechanical snuffers which contained a concealed spring to keep the box shut. Many ingenious improvements, some less practical than others, followed. Most relied on a spring, but in 1810 Samuel Hobday, a snuffer maker of Birmingham, patented a pair of snuffers which had a concealed lever which worked by an eccentric on the hinge. Eight years later he patented a simpler type which had neither spring nor lever and this was widely adopted by other makers. Improvements to snuffers continued until the early 1840s, but by then significant improvements to both candles and wicks had reduced the need for snuffing.

A label for Price's composite snuffless candles of c.1860 contrasting an old guttering tallow candle (left) in the hands of an old woman and the modern snuffless candle, which, it was claimed did not drop grease – even when carried by a careless young girl!

A view inside the works of 'Prices Patent Candle Company' in 1849, showing the large steam boiling vats which were used to separate the fatty acids from the lime soap in the saponification process.

NINETEENTH-CENTURY DEVELOPMENTS

Between the 1820s and the 1850s, candles were vastly improved by a series of far reaching scientific discoveries. New candle materials were introduced and the industry transformed from one based on traditional craft skills to a major manufacturing industry. The first significant discovery was the result of the research of a French chemist, Michel Eugene Chevreul. He began researching into the nature of tallow in 1811. Two years later he announced that tallow was not, as previously supposed, a single, uniform substance, but a compound which could be separated. He demonstrated that the inflammable nature of tallow was largely due to the presence of two fatty acids, stearic acid and oelic acid. In tallow these were combined with glycerine to form a neutral compound. In 1825, in collaboration with Gay Lussac, a fellow scientist, he applied his research to the commercial production of a new type of

candle. By removing the glycerine, which is relatively uninflammable, he obtained a new substance which he named *stearine*. This was harder than natural tallow and burned with a brighter flame. Chevreul and Lussac subjected tallow to the action of a strong alkali, such as potash or soda, which released the glycerine and combined with the fatty acids to produce a *soap*. It was then necessary to break the soap down so that the fatty acids could be freed and this was achieved by treating it with dilute sulphuric acid. As the liquid oelic acid gave the resulting mass an unpleasant brown colour and greasy texture, it was carefully squeezed out by pressing. The remaining hard white mass, stearine, made excellent candles, but Chevreul's venture ended in failure, partly because of the high cost of using potash. Commercial success came to another Frenchman, de Milly, who substituted the much cheaper lime for potash, and he

ABOVE: *The hydraulic press room at Price's Vauxhall factory, about 1850. Powerful steam-powered hydraulic presses were used to extract the liquid oelic acid from the stearine.*

BELOW: *A scene of bustling activity inside the candle moulding department at Prices. The moulding machines were moved along railway lines as they went through the various stages of production, from heating the moulds to extracting the finished candles.*

A moulding machine. The workman is in the act of separating the finished candles and simultaneously rewicking the moulds by depressing the lever with his right hand.

began manufacturing his candles, named *bougies de l'étoile* in 1831. Within a few years, de Milly's process of *lime saponification* became established in England, but the candles were still expensive and at first made little progress.

Nevertheless, developments continued apace. Chevreul's initial discovery concerning tallow was soon followed by the realisation that solid inflammable fats, similar to stearine, could be extracted from vegetable oils. In 1829 James Soames patented a process for obtaining coconut oil from the fruit of the coconut palm. Using hydraulic pressure, coconut oil could be extracted with little difficulty. In 1830 Soames's patent was purchased by two tallow merchants, William Wilson and Benjamin Lancaster, who, under the name E. Price and Company, began production the same year. The name Price, which was to become so closely associated

with British candle manufacture, was that of an aunt of Lancaster's who had no active involvement in the industry. In 1836, Dr John Hemple and Henry Blundell patented the use of a substance called *palmatine* for candlemaking, derived from palm oil. At first the impact of these discoveries was lessened by various problems. Price's coconut oil candles were soft and tended to gutter like ordinary tallow candles and the candles made from palmatine by Blundell and Spence gave a good light but were of a dark colour and never came into general use.

Then, in 1840, E. Price and Company introduced a new *snuffless* candle to coincide with Queen Victoria's wedding to Prince Albert. Made from a combination of coconut oil and stearine, these candles were termed *composite*. They sold for a shilling a pound and so they were cheap enough to compete with tallow candles. But the composite material was also hard enough to do away with the thick troublesome wicks associated with cheap tallow. Instead they were fitted with *plaited wicks*, which had a natural inclination to curl over and burn away on the edge of the flame. Plaited wicks were invented in France by Cambacères in 1820. By 1830 some British makers had taken them up, although at first they were suitable only for wax and tallow candles. But after 1840, with the rapid spread of cheap composite candles, the use of plaited wicks greatly increased. The wicks were usually pickled in various solutions, commonly boracic acid, to retard combustion and help in the destruction of the ash, but snuffers were still needed to trim the wicks of ordinary tallow candles, which, still the cheapest, were made in the twentieth century.

The reduction in the price of composite stearine was the product of continuing research into improving materials and processes. E. Price and Company were particularly prominent in this respect and in 1843 perfected a method of refining fats by distillation. This was considerably more economical than lime saponification, yielding 75 per cent of candle material as against 50 per cent for the older process. No other method gave such a high yield and the process became widely adopted. Distillation was also suitable for obtaining

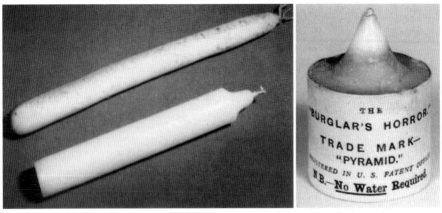

LEFT: *A moulded paraffin wax candle (lower) compared with a tallow dip (upper).*
RIGHT: *'Pyramid' night light, c.1900, manufactured by Prices Patent Candle Company. Night lights were short squat candles with small wicks designed to burn for six, eight or ten hours. Prices had almost a monopoly of the production, turning out over thirty-two million in 1878.*

a good quality candle material from palm oil and from the 1840s the use of this oil increased rapidly.

A candle material of mineral origin was added to the known animal and vegetable sources when *paraffin wax* was discovered. This substance was first isolated by Reichenbach in 1830 but did not become available in large quantities until the 1850s. In 1850 the scientist James Young perfected a method of obtaining paraffin wax by the distillation of oil shales. The following year, at the Great Exhibition, a French manufacturer, Masse, Tribouillet & Company, exhibited paraffin wax candles made by distilling bituminous schist. In 1857, the first paraffin wax candles appeared on the British market. They were made by J. C. and J. Field of the Lambeth Marsh candle works, an old established firm of wax chandlers who could trace their foundation to 1508. Paraffin wax candles were the equal of beeswax and spermaceti for brightness, hardness and gloss. Initially the chief source was *torbanite,* an oil shale found in the Lothian region of Scotland. Subsequently paraffin was obtained from petroleum, and following the discovery of enormous oilfields in Pennsylvania, USA, in 1859, cheap plentiful supplies reached British manufacturers. Combining cheapness with quality, paraffin wax

candles had largely supplanted rival types by 1900. Nevertheless, a small amount of stearine was added to paraffin wax candles to harden them. The old tallow dip also continued to be made for use in industrial premises where they were found to be more durable than mould candles through being made of many layers.

The technical advances in candlemaking were accompanied by the rise of large manufacturers in London and elsewhere, capable of utilising their full commercial potential. The industry also benefited from the repeal of the excise duties in 1831. Candles had been taxed from 1709, and throughout the eighteenth and early nineteenth centuries chandlers had been subjected to many oppressive regulations and the constant supervision of excise officers. With the removal of these laws, candlemakers were free to expand unhindered. Large factories were established producing millions of candles each year in many different varieties, including coloured candles made with vegetable dyes and fancy patterns. By 1851 E. Price and Company, which had become the famous Prices Patent Candle Company, employed over nine hundred men in their two factories at Vauxhall and Battersea, London. The company had its own extensive coco-palm plantations in Ceylon (Sri Lanka) and in 1851 was producing one hundred tons of candles per week; in 1854 they opened a third factory at Bromborough Pool on the river Mersey.

Such prodigious figures would not have been possible without the development of candle moulding machines. The earliest recorded improvement on the basic hand frame is found in 1796 in the patent of Joseph Sampson, who added a continuous wick. This feature later became standard on candle machines as it cut out the time-consuming operation of rewicking each mould by hand. In 1801 Thomas Binns added a water jacket to the frame, which was connected to hot and cold water supplies. By admitting cold water to the moulds, the time taken for the candles to harden was considerably reduced. The water jacket also facilitated a fine degree of control over the temperature at which the candle material was moulded. This was useful in combating crystallisation, which could spoil the appearance of candles, particularly stearine, spermaceti and paraffin wax. By setting the temperature to just a little above the congealing point of the material, the cooling time was reduced and crystallisation avoided. The result was the production of candles with an attractive hard gloss. In the 1820s and 1830s two leading candle machine makers, Joseph Morgan and Joseph Tuck, added movable pistons to their machines. These were operated by a lever and simultaneously ejected the candles and rewicked the moulds for the next batch.

Following the introduction of paraffin wax candles, the pace of inventions lessened, but in the years immediately after the mid nineteenth century the candle industry was probably at its peak. Cheap but bright candles, far superior to the traditional tallow dip, were widely available. The candle remained the most usual form of artificial lighting in most homes, although alternatives were developing and multiplying. From the late eighteenth century, improved oil lamps burning colza oil had appeared in the drawing rooms of the wealthy. Not long afterwards, gas was proved to be a practical form of domestic lighting. But gas was dependent on nearby gasworks and rarely reached the countryside.

Packaging label post-dating 1910, when Clarke's night-light business was taken over by Prices.

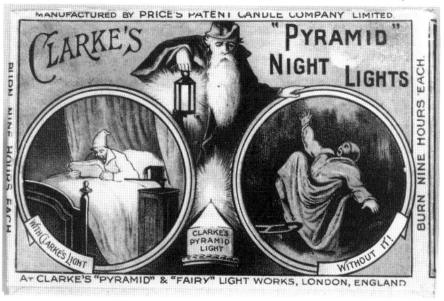

Colza oil was expensive and this restricted the use of the lamps. Only with the introduction of kerosene or paraffin oil, available in large quantities from the 1850s, was an alternative found that, in terms of both economy and light power, was superior to the candle. By the 1860s cheap paraffin lamps costing less than a shilling were flooding the market. Within a few decades, the electric light came to resolve one of man's oldest problems, once and for all. Gradually, the candle was eclipsed. In Britain, the consumption of candles fell from about 45,000 tons per annum in 1916 to 7,000 tons in 1959.

CANDLEHOLDERS

Candleholders have ranged from spectacular chandeliers of cut glass to crude holders of wood and iron. Whilst expensive chandeliers, candelabra and highly decorative wall sconces were generally confined to the rich, candlesticks were to be found at every social level and therefore made of every possible material. Candlesticks made of silver and other fine materials such as porcelain and cut glass were confined to the rich. Below the level of the aristocracy and gentry, ownership of silver, for example, rarely extended beyond a few silver spoons and the odd tankard. Much useful information as to the types of candlesticks used by the broad middle ranks of society can be derived from probate inventories, which list household contents and survive in large numbers for the period roughly between 1550 and 1750. Occasionally inventories list pottery and wooden candlesticks, but their numbers are insignificant compared to those ascribed to base metals – brass, iron and pewter. For most people, a candlestick was simply a commonplace household utensil, as basic as the kettles and pans in the kitchen.

Brass candlesticks occur frequently in inventories of the sixteenth and seventeenth centuries, even though English makers were at that time largely dependent on foreign supplies. Only after 1702, with the founding of a brassworks at Baptist Mills, Bristol, was good quality English brass available in large quantities. The largest proportion of Bristol brass found its way to Birmingham, which by the early eighteenth century was already established as the chief centre of small, finished brass goods. By 1770 there were seven specialist candlestick makers there and, although brass candlesticks were made elsewhere, Birmingham remained pre-eminent in their manufacture throughout the nineteenth century.

Pewtering was dominated by the London makers, but pewterers were also active in many provincial towns. Candlesticks were a regular part of their range of goods and pewter examples figure in large numbers in inventories of the sixteenth and seventeenth centuries. But, shortly after the beginning of the eighteenth century, their numbers diminish markedly. This is but one symptom of the general decline of pewter in the face of growing com-

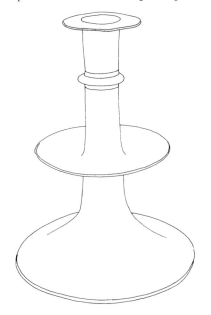

A pewter candlestick of the mid seventeenth century, with trumpet-shaped base and wide drip pan.

ABOVE, LEFT: *Brass table candlesticks were produced in the eighteenth and nineteenth centuries in a very great variety of patterns. The combinations of decorative knops on the stems varied with each manufacturer. Few candlesticks were made with makers' marks, though this rare example was manufactured by John Moffat, brassfounder, candlestick and snuffer maker of the Scotland Works, Birmingham, between c.1849 and 1860.*

ABOVE, CENTRE: *A typical tin-plate candlestick with slide ejector.*

ABOVE, RIGHT: *Tinplate candle-stick, probably of mid-nineteenth-century date, with a slide ejector and wide drip pan, recalling seventeenth-century patterns.*

RIGHT: *A combined rushlight and candle bracket of wrought iron, which could be driven into a wall or beam.*

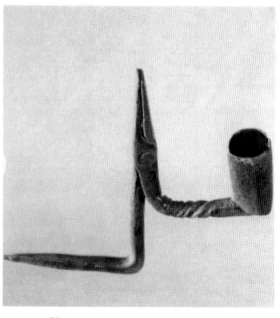

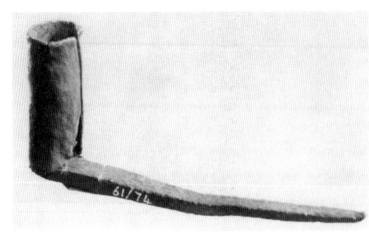

A crude wrought iron candle holder with a spike for fixing into a wall or rafter.

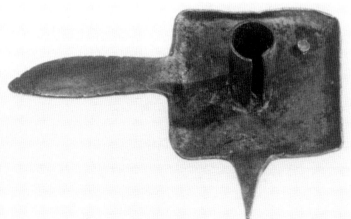

A blacksmith-made iron chamberstick.

Chamberstick with a long flat handle resembling a frying pan, made from sheet brass.

LEFT: *A candlestick made of a flat strip of iron, wound in the form of a hollow spiral with a wooden base. A thin iron strap is set through the spiral and could be moved up as the candle burned shorter.*

RIGHT: *Sheet brass chambersticks are sometimes found bearing the name of a school, almshouse or other institution. This example, dated 1811, is inscribed 'Guild Hall Bristol'.*

petition from rival trades for the market in tableware and household utensils. Chief amongst these was the burgeoning tinplate industry. The use of thin sheets of iron coated with tin, to retard rusting, was known in the middle ages. The production of good quality tinplate, however, involved a number of complex processes and, although there was a modest rise in the use of tin utensils in the late seventeenth century, this was largely accountable to tinplate imported from Germany. During the early eighteenth century tinplate mills began to be established in various parts of Britain and the use of tinplate utensils, including candlesticks, increased rapidly. Tinplate candlesticks remained common throughout the eighteenth and nineteenth centuries. They were always extremely plain and contrasted with pewter and brass candlesticks, which

Elm chamberstick made by George Lailey, wood turner of Bucklebury Common, Berkshire, in the 1930s. It was originally sold for between one shilling and sixpence and two shillings.

often carried the decorative lines of silver. Most humble were wrought iron candlesticks made by local blacksmiths. These lacked sufficient intrinsic value to be recorded in inventories but were widely used in poorer homes.

Inventories say little about the shape of candlesticks, but fortunately sufficient examples which can be dated survive to complement the documentary evidence. In the middle ages candlesticks were usually provided with a spike called a *pricket* on which the candle was impaled. This arrangement worked well with large candles but was unsuitable for the small tallow dip. With the increasing domestic use of candles in the sixteenth century, the pricket was replaced by the more familiar socket. In the sixteenth and seventeenth centuries most candlesticks were also supplied with a substantial grease pan. This was large enough to catch the extra drips caused by a candle burning away rapidly, or *swealing,* as it was carried through a draught.

Towards the end of the seventeenth century, a growing distinction emerged between *table candlesticks* and those designed to be carried around. From about 1680 table candlesticks lost the large drip catcher in favour of a narrow flange around the socket: this was quite adequate to catch the drips of a guttering candle providing it was not moved. From around the same time, inventories occasionally refer to 'hand candlesticks'. These later became more familiarly known as *chambersticks.* The usual form had a squat stem, set in a wide pan with a ring handle, although some had long flat handles resembling frying pans. The majority of chambersticks were made of brass. The earlier ones were cast, but following the introduction of improved methods of stamping sheet metal after 1770 many were made from thin sheet brass. In the nineteenth century large numbers of cheap chambersticks were made from mass-produced materials such as Staffordshire earthenware, pressed glass and, later in the century, enamelled iron. In 1844 a tinned iron chamberstick complete with snuffers and extinguisher could be bought in London for 6d — the same price as a pound of the cheapest tallow dips. More expensive were those with

ABOVE: *Reading candlesticks were made with sockets that could be adjusted on a vertical stem to keep the light at the same height. They also had metal shades with a japanned (oven-baked) white interior to reflect the light down and to conceal the flame from the eyes. In 1844 Thomas Webster claimed that they were economical as one candle gave as much light as two without shades.*

A 'save-all', redrawn from Thomas Webster's 'Encyclopedia of Domestic Economy', 1844.

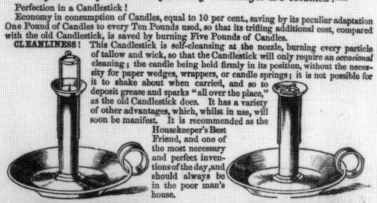

CLEANLINESS, ECONOMY, AND COMFORT,

SECURED BY THE

PATENT ECONOMIC CANDLESTICK,

By the use of which the following advantages are obtained:—

Perfection in a Candlestick!

Economy in consumption of Candles, equal to 10 per cent., saving by its peculiar adaptation One Pound of Candles to every Ten Pounds used, so that its trifling additional cost, compared with the old Candlestick, is saved by burning Five Pounds of Candles.

CLEANLINESS! This Candlestick is self-cleansing at the nozzle, burning every particle of tallow and wick, so that the Candlestick will only require an *occasional* cleaning; the candle being held firmly in its position, without the necessity for paper wedges, wrappers, or candle springs; it is not possible for it to shake about when carried, and so to deposit grease and sparks "all over the place," as the old Candlestick does. It has a variety of other advantages, which, whilst in use, will soon be manifest. It is recommended as the Housekeeper's Best Friend, and one of the most necessary and perfect inventions of the day, and should always be in the poor man's house.

HENRY LOVERIDGE & Co., Sole Manufacturers,
MERRIDALE WORKS, WOLVERHAMPTON.

ABOVE: *Candles were sold in so many different sizes that it was often impossible to fit one into a socket without wedging it with paper. Many patents were taken out for adjustable sockets, but according to this advertisement from 'The Ironmonger', 1861, Henry Loveridge had found an easier answer. The alternative adopted by many candlemakers was to fit fins to the end of the candle to ensure a tight fit.*

BELOW: *Before the introduction of the phosphorus-tipped match in the 1830s, the only convenient way to make a light was by striking a flint (right) against a steel (left). Tinder boxes, such as this example made of brass, usually included a candle socket on the lid so it could also be used as a portable candlestick.*

deep fretted sides and a glass shade to protect the flame from draughts.

Removing the candle stump from the socket was often a difficult and laborious task. In the sixteenth and seventeenth centuries many candlesticks were made with a hole in the side of the socket so that a sharp instrument could be poked through to dislodge the remains. In the mid seventeenth century a push-up device was introduced as an easier way of ejecting the stump. This consisted of a metal plate, held tight inside the stem with a spring. By moving a thumb piece on the side of the stem, the plate could be moved up to push out the stump. This device was also used to regulate the height of the flame. Around 1700, the central push-rod ejector was introduced. The rod ran through the hollow stem of a candlestick and was pushed up by a button under the base. Both push-up and slide ejectors were widely used on brass and tinplate candlesticks in the eighteenth and nineteenth centuries. In 1842 Thomas Clive, a Birmingham ironfounder, patented a push-up device which was worked by a rack and pinion turned by a little winder, similar to those of oil lamps. Clive's invention, however, was never widely adopted. Once ejected, the candle stump was used up in economical households on a *save-all*. This usually took the form of a small cup with three projecting wires, clips or a central spike, on which the stump was fixed.

Candlesticks specially designed for reading or writing by were made with metal shades. The shade served the dual function of reflecting the light downwards and hiding the glare of the flame. They were widely used in offices in the eighteenth and nineteenth centuries and typically consisted of a vertical rod, which supported the shade, and one or two adjustable sockets. As the candle burned away, the sockets were moved up on the rod to maintain the height of the flame. After 1830 several manufacturers produced a reading candlestick with a hollow stem or column in which the candle was placed. A coiled spring underneath the candle kept it pressed up against an opening in the top of the column, so that it always burned at the same height. They were usually known as *candle lamps* and

Candle lamp made by William Palmer of Clerkenwell, London, about 1840. First patented in 1832, the lamps burned special 'metallic wick' candles which were made so as not to require snuffing.

ABOVE, LEFT: *A candle screen used in bedrooms for burning rush candles – an early form of night light – which had wicks made of rushes. These were pierced at one end to make a loop and then made by dipping like tallow candles. In 'Great Expectations', first published in 1861, Charles Dickens describes how these rush candles burned in a 'high tin tower perforated with round holes [and] made a startlingly wide awake pattern on the walls'. They were also called 'thousand eye' lanterns although this one actually has just 144 holes.*

ABOVE, RIGHT: *Japanned iron and horn lantern once used by a country parson in Berkshire and Hampshire. Side handle and fluted cap over the roof.*

RIGHT: *Tinplate and horn lantern typical of farmhouse use; note the dormer in the roof. Nineteenth or early twentieth century.*

CANDLE HORN AND CAMP LANTERNS.

128

1895. Tin Colza Lamps, with Hollow Bottom to fit on Candle Holder in Lantern 6/6 per doz.

5750. Japanned Candle Lantern, 5½ × 3½-in. 10/0 doz.

5751. Japanned Candle Lantern. 6 × 3½-in. ... 11/6 doz. 120/0 per gross. **5752.** 7½ × 4½-in. 21/6 doz.

5753. Square Tin Candle Lanterns, with Hinge Tops. No Guards. Size 3 6½ × 4-in. ... 15/0 doz. " 4 7½ × 4½-in. ... 18/6 " " 5 8 × 4½-in. 21/6 "

5754. Square Tin Candle Lantern, with Hinged Top Wire Guards. Size 2 6½ × 3½-in. ... 16/6 doz. " 3 6½ × 3½-in. ... 20/0 " " 5 8 × 4½-in. ... 27/0 "

5755. Patent Square Tin Candle Lantern. No Soldering. Size 1 6½ × 3½ ... 20/6 doz. " 2 7½ × 4½ ... 26/6 " " 3 8½ × 5 ... 33/0 "

5756. Bright Tin Candle Lantern, 8 × 5-in., 21/6 doz.

Stable Lantern, with Door and Wire Guards. Glass Panels. **5757.** 7 × 4-in. ... 18/0 doz. **5758.** 8½ × 5-in. ... 26/0 " **5759.** 10 × 6-in. ... 35/0 " Also Nested for Export. 6/8 per set, or 74/0 doz. sets.

Japanned Candle Lantern, with fixed Handle at top. **5760.** 6½ × 4-in. ... 17/0 per doz. **5761.** 7½ × 4½-in. ... 22/6 per doz.

Horn Candle Lantern. With Wire Guards and Patent Candle Grip. **5762.** Dia. 5½-in. 34/0 doz. **5763.** " 6-in., 42/0 " **5764.** " 6½-in., 51/0 "

5765. Horn Candle Lantern. 7½-in. diameter, with Stamped Dormered Top. 68/0 doz.

CAMP LANTERNS.

Made to burn either CANDLES, COLZA OIL, or PARAFFIN.

(No. 2 Barton Burner.)

Japanned and Glazed.

In Japanned Tin Case, complete.

5768. Triangular Shape. 14/0 each, complete.

5769. Square Shape. 14/0 each, complete.

Bright Tin Candle Lantern. **6983.** 9 × 4-in. 15/6 doz. **6984.** 11 × 5-in. 22/6 " **6985.** 13 × 6½-in. 30/0 "

Range of lanterns available in the lamp catalogue of S. P. Catterson and Sons Ltd., 1907-8.

ABOVE, LEFT: *Lantern with glass panes. Used at Hurst, Berkshire, in the mid nineteenth century.*
ABOVE, RIGHT: *Lantern with glass panes. Used at Glastonbury, Somerset.*

were often fitted with etched glass shades similar to those found on oil and gas lamps. The shade helped to induce a strong supply of oxygen to the flame and so these lamps burned brightly. They enjoyed a measure of success during the 1840s and 1850s, but they were difficult to clean and their popularity waned with the introduction of paraffin lamps from the late 1850s.

Hand lanterns used to protect candles from wind and rain out of doors date from at least early medieval times. For wealthy travellers there were elaborate folding lanterns but the everyday lantern was simply a container, either cylindrical or rectangular, of sheet iron or brass, fitted with a carrying handle. The roof was usually conical and made with holes to supply air to the candle; these holes

were frequently protected by a fluted cap or by small dormers. The handle was either attached to the side like a tankard or fixed to the roof.

For centuries lanterns were often fitted with panels of thin, translucent horn; others, however, were made without windows, just pierced sides which emitted only tiny points of light; they were probably only ever intended as safety lights to be hung from obstructions which were not visible at night. From the seventeenth century some lanterns were fitted with a bull's-eye glass, a by-product of making window glass. In the nineteenth century lanterns were increasingly fitted with thin glass panels, but on farms horn lanterns were preferred for if kicked over by a horse or cow they were less likely to break and set fire to surrounding straw or hay. From the 1870s the candle lantern began to give way to the hurricane lamp burning paraffin but horn lanterns, valued for their safety, were still being made in the 1920s.

FURTHER READING

Andre, G. G. (editor). *Spon's Encyclopedia of the Industrial Arts, Manufactures and Commercial Products.* Spon, 18/9.

Ashley, Robert. *The Rushlight and Related Holders: A Regional View.* Ashley Publications, Marlborough, Wiltshire, 2001.

Bowers, B. *Lengthening the Day: A History of Lighting Technology.* Oxford University Press, 1998.

Caspall, John. *Making Fire and Light in the Home pre 1820.* Antique Collectors' Club, 1987.

Cossons, N. *Rees's Manufacturing Industries (1819–20).* David & Charles, 1972.

Dummelow, John. *The Wax Chandlers of London.* Phillimore, 1973.

Gentle, R., and Field, R. *English Domestic Brass.* Elek, 1975.

Michaelis, R. F. *Old Domestic Base Metal Candlesticks.* Antique Collectors' Club, 1978.

Moore, J. S. *The Goods and Chattels of Our Forefathers.* Phillimore, 1976.

O'Dea, W. T. *The Social History of Lighting.* Routledge & Kegan Paul, 1958.

Seymour Lindsay, J. *Iron and Brass Implements of the English House.* Medici, 1927.

Steer, F. W. *Farm and Cottage Inventories of Mid Essex 1635–1749.* Phillimore, 1969.

Trinder, B., and Cox, J. *Yeomen and Colliers in Telford.* Phillimore, 1980.

Webster, T. *An Encyclopedia of Domestic Economy.* Longman, 1844.

Wills, G. *Candlesticks.* David & Charles, 1974.

PLACES TO VISIT

Many museums have candlesticks on display. Some of particular interest are listed here. Intending visitors are advised to find out the opening times before making a special journey.

Birmingham Museum and Art Gallery, Chamberlain Square, Birmingham B3 3DH. Telephone: 0121 235 2834. Website: www.bmag.org.uk

Blaise Castle House Museum, Henbury Road, Henbury, Bristol BS10 7QS. Telephone: 0117 903 9818. Website: www.bristol-city.gov.uk/mus/blaise

Blists Hill Open Air Museum, Legges Way, Madeley, Telford, Shropshire TF8 7AW. Telephone: 01952 586063 or 583003. Website: www.ironbridge.org.uk

Carisbrooke Castle Museum, Carisbrooke, Newport, Isle of Wight PO30 1XY. Telephone: 01983 523112. Website: www.carisbrookecastlemuseum.org.uk

Ceredigion Museum, The Coliseum, Terrace Road, Aberystwyth, Ceredigion SY23 2AQ. Telephone: 01970 633087. Website: www.ceredigion.gov.uk/coliseum

Museum of St Albans, Hatfield Road, St Albans, Hertfordshire AL1 3RR. Telephone: 01727 819340. Website: www.stalbansmuseums.org.uk

Museum of Welsh Life, St Fagans, Cardiff CF5 6XB. Telephone: 029 2057 3500. Website: www.nmgw.ac.uk

Number 1, Royal Crescent, Bath BA1 2LR. Telephone: 01225 428126. Website: www.bath-preservation-trust.org.uk

Powysland Museum and Montgomery Canal Centre, Canal Wharf, Severn Street, Welshpool, Powys SY21 7AQ. Telephone: 01938 554656. Website: www.powys.gov.uk

The Red House Museum, Quay Road, Christchurch, Dorset BH23 1BU. Telephone: 01202 482860. Website: www.hants.gov.uk/museums

Science Museum, Exhibition Road, South Kensington, London SW7 2DD. Telephone: 0870 870 4771. Website: www.sciencemuseum.org.uk

The Stewartry Museum, St Mary Street, Kirkcudbright, Dumfries and Galloway DG6 4AG. Telephone: 01557 331643. Website: www.kirkcudbright.co.uk

York Castle Museum, Eye of York, Tower Street, York YO1 9RY. Telephone: 01904 650333. Website: www.yorkcastlemuseum.org.uk

AUSTRALIA

Sovereign Hill, Ballarat, Victoria 3350, Australia. Telephone: (00613) 5331 1944. Website: www.sovereignhill.com.au